DATE DUE

Demco, Inc. 38-293

WHY DOES THE MOON CHANGE SHAPE?

MELISSA STEWART

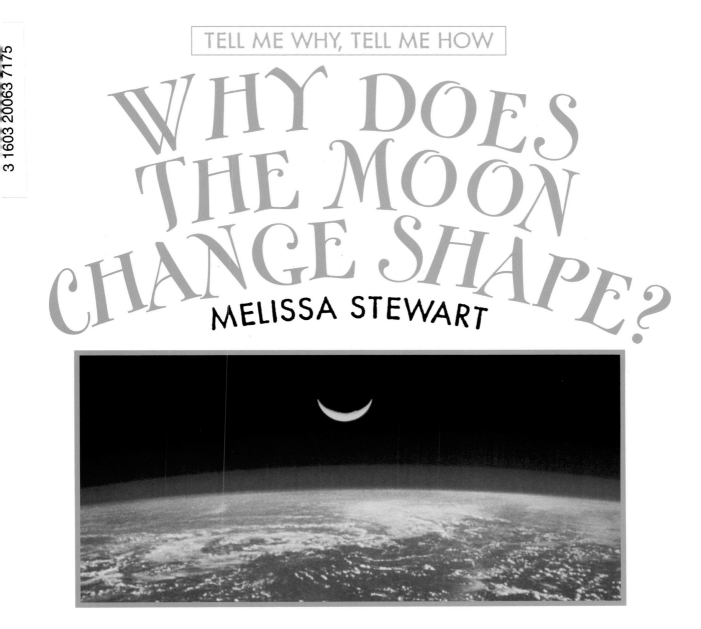

 **Marshall Cavendish**
Benchmark
New York

Marshall Cavendish Benchmark
99 White Plains Road
Tarrytown, NY 10591-5502
www.marshallcavendish.us

Library of Congress Cataloging-in-Publication Data

Stewart, Melissa.
Why does the moon change shape? / by Melissa Stewart.
p. cm. — (Tell me why, tell me how)
Summary: "Provides comprehensive information on the moon and the phases it goes through in a month"—
Provided by publisher.
Includes index.
ISBN 978-0-7614-2921-0
1. Moon—Juvenile literature. 2. Moon—Phases—Juvenile literature. I.
Title. II. Series.

QB582.S74 2009
523.3—dc22

2007025247

Photo research by Candlepants Incorporated

Cover Photo: Jan Hoglund / Jupiter Images

The photographs in this book are used by permission and through the courtesy of:
Getty Images: Pete Turner, 1. *Peter Arnold Inc.*: Astrofoto, 4; BIOS Mafart-Renodier Alain, 5. *Photo Researchers Inc.*: Mary Evans Picture Library, 6; Shigemi Numazawa / Atlas Photo Bank, 7; John Sanford, 22; Steve A. Munsinger, 23; Larry Landolfi, 24; NASA / LMSAL / G.L. Slater & G.A. Linford / Science Source, 18. *Jupiter Images*: NASA/ Stock Image, 8; Galaxy Contact, 20; John Sanford, 26; Jan Hoglund, . *Shutterstock*: 9, 16. *Corbis*: Tim Kiusalaas, 10; Denis Scott, 12; Corbis, 13, 14; Craig Tuttle, 15; Roger Ressmeyer, 19; Darrell Gulin, 25. *Digital Railroad*: Tom & Therisa Stack/Tom Stack & Associates / drr.net, 11.

Editor: Joy Bean
Publisher: Michelle Bisson
Art Director: Anahid Hamparian
Series Designer: Alex Ferrari

Printed in Malaysia
1 3 5 6 4 2

CONTENTS

The Mysterious Moon – 5

Our Place in Space – 9

The Moon in Motion – 13

Let There Be Light – 19

Why Does the Moon
Change Shape? – 23

Activity – 28

Glossary – 29

Find Out More – 31

Index – 32

People have always enjoyed looking at the Moon and stars. Today, small portable telescopes can give us a better view than ever before.

The Mysterious Moon

For as long as people have lived on Earth, they have asked questions about the bright lights that fill the nighttime sky. What causes them? How far away are they? Why do they move from night to night?

The Moon is so bright that we can often see it at dusk. Sometimes we can even see it in the middle of the day.

For thousands of years, the Moon has been the most mysterious nighttime object of all. It is the largest object in the night sky, and it is the brightest. What amazed ancient people

This 600-year-old drawing shows two European astronomers studying the Moon and recording their observations in a notebook.

the most is how the Moon's shape is constantly changing. Sometimes it looks like a full bright circle. Other times, only a tiny sliver appears.

It did not take ancient people long to realize that the Moon's changes, or **phases**, follow a regular pattern. The Moon's phases repeat themselves every twenty-nine or thirty days. If you watch the Moon every night for about a month, you can see all its phases.

At the beginning of each **cycle**, people on Earth cannot see the Moon at all. After a few days, a tiny sliver of light appears in the nighttime sky. Each night, the Moon looks a little larger. After a week, it looks like half of a circle. And about a week after that, a full round disk brightens the night sky.

But then the Moon starts to shrink. Each night it gets a bit smaller. After about a week, the Moon looks like half of a circle. And a week after that, the Moon disappears completely. But a few days later, a tiny sliver of light returns. This cycle has repeated itself for billions of years.

This series of photos shows what the Moon looks like during each night of its cycle. You can see one half of the Moon lit up on Day 7, a Full Moon on Day 14, and the other half of the Moon lit up on Day 21.

Now I Know!

How long is a moon cycle?

Twenty-nine or thirty days.

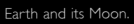

Earth and its Moon.

Our Place in Space

Earth is one of eight planets in our **solar system**. The other planets are Mercury, Venus, Mars, Jupiter, Saturn, Uranus, and Neptune.

All eight planets **orbit**, or move around, a star called the Sun. A **year** is the amount of time it takes a planet to circle the Sun once. Earth completes the trip in about 365 days, so an Earth year is 365 days long. That is the amount of time between your last birthday and your next birthday.

The Sun and eight planets in our solar system, showing their relative size to each other. From left: Mercury, Venus, Earth, Mars, Jupiter, Saturn, Uranus, and Neptune.

Mercury is the closest planet to the Sun. It makes one full orbit in just eighty-eight days, so a year on Mercury is much shorter than a year on Earth. Neptune is the farthest planet from the Sun. It takes Neptune 165 Earth years to circle the Sun. That is a really long time to wait between birthdays!

Planets are not the only objects that orbit the Sun. Thousands of smaller, rocky chunks called **asteroids** and **dwarf planets** do, too. Most asteroids follow paths located between Mars and Jupiter. Dwarf planets, such as Pluto, are larger than asteroids. Their orbits are located beyond Neptune.

Comets are small icy objects that orbit the Sun. Their orbital paths around the Sun are long and thin, like a cucumber.

Planets, asteroids, dwarf planets, and

Each planet in our solar system follows a specific path as it orbits the Sun.

10

comets do not fly off into space because the Sun's **gravity** is always tugging on these smaller objects. Their forward movement is perfectly balanced with the pull of the Sun's gravity.

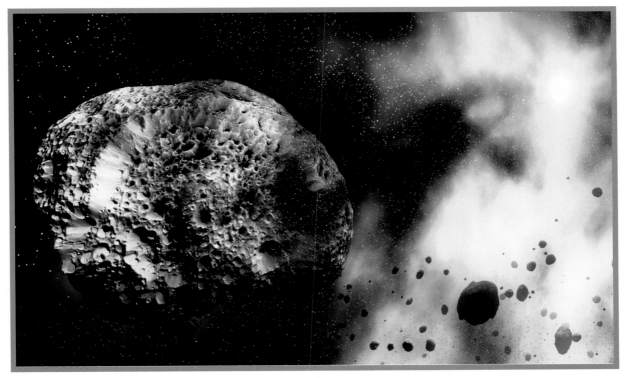

Asteroids are small, rocky objects that orbit the Sun.

The Sun is a huge, massive object at the center of our solar system. Its gravity controls the orbits of planets more than a billion miles away.

The Moon in Motion

The Sun is not the only object in our solar system with enough gravitational pull to attract smaller bodies. Six planets—Earth, Mars, Jupiter, Saturn, Uranus, and Neptune—have smaller objects orbiting them. So do a few asteroids and dwarf planets. These smaller objects are moons.

Jupiter has at least sixty moons. The four largest ones are shown in this collage of images taken by the Voyager 1 spacecraft. They are Callisto (bottom left), Europa (center), Ganymede (bottom center) and Io (right).

Scientists have identified at least sixty moons circling Jupiter. Saturn probably has even more. But Mars has just two moons, and Earth has only one.

Earth's Moon is closer to Earth than any other object in space. Still, it took Apollo astronauts traveling at rocket speed about four days to reach the Moon in the late 1960s and early 1970s. The Moon is about 238,860 miles (384,400 kilometers) from Earth. That is almost one hundred times farther than the

A total of six Apollo spacecraft carried people to the Moon. The astronauts returned with photos, rock samples, and amazing stories of what they saw as they cruised around in lunar rovers.

distance between New York, New York, and Los Angeles, California.

It takes the Moon about twenty-seven days to complete one full orbit around Earth. That means it circles our planet about twelve times each year.

As the Moon orbits Earth, it also **rotates**, or spins like a top. Earth rotates too. Our planet takes about twenty-four

When Earth's one and only Moon is full, it brightens up the nighttime sky.

hours—or one full **day**—to complete one rotation. The Moon spins much more slowly. It rotates just once during each twenty-seven day orbit.

As Earth spins, different areas of the planet face the Sun. It is daytime in the places that are facing the Sun. That is why days are bright and sunny. It is nighttime on the part of Earth facing away from the Sun. That is why it is dark at night.

The amount of time it takes the Moon to rotate is the same as the time the Moon takes to orbit Earth, so people on Earth always see the

In this image of Earth and the Moon, you can see part of the far side of the moon, the half of the Moon that never faces Earth.

same side of the Moon. Scientists call the side we see the near side. When the near side of the Moon is lit up by the Sun, we see a full, bright circle. When the far side of the Moon is fully lit up by the Sun, we cannot see the Moon at all.

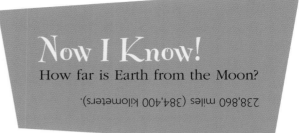

Now I Know!

How far is Earth from the Moon?

238,860 miles (384,400 kilometers).

This x-ray image of the Sun shows some of the fiery gases it sends out into space.

Let There Be Light

The Sun is a star—a giant ball of boiling gases. The temperature at the center of the Sun is 27 million degrees Fahrenheit (15 million degrees Celsius). The gases inside the Sun are so hot that it glows. The Sun is not the biggest star in the Universe, but it looks the brightest in the sky to us because it is the closest.

During some parts of the year, we can see Venus, Mars, Jupiter, and Saturn as bright, steadily shining dots of light in the night sky. But these planets do not produce their own

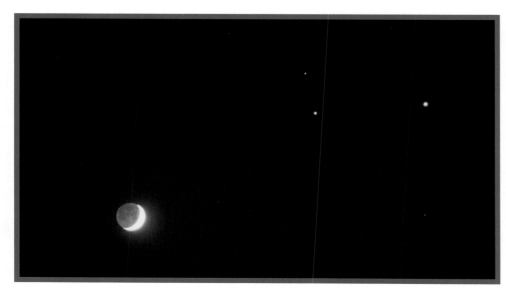

The night sky as seen from Earth shows the Moon in its crescent phase and three planets—Mars (top), Jupiter (middle), and Venus (right).

Apollo astronauts took this photo of the Moon's rocky surface. The large holes, or craters, show that, over millions of years, many space rocks have crashed into the Moon.

light. The light we see when we look at them comes from the Sun. As the Sun's rays hit a planet, some of the light bounces off the planet's surfaces and travels back into space. When some of that **reflected** light reaches our eyes, the planet seems to glow. The Moon reflects the Sun's light, too.

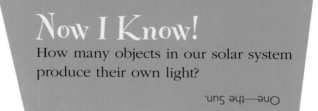

We know from astronauts and space vehicles visiting the Moon that it is made of solid rock. There is no source of light on the Moon. We can only see the Moon when the Sun is shining on it, and then that light is reflected off the Moon's surface and into our eyes. The Moon is much smaller than Venus, Mars, Jupiter, and Saturn, but it looks bigger and brighter to us because it is much closer to Earth than those planets are.

The phases of the moon,
from bottom moving
counter clockwise.

Full Moon

Gibbous

Gibbous

First Quarter

Last Quarter

Crescent

Crescent

New Moon

Why Does the Moon Change Shape?

During any twenty-nine or thirty day period, the Moon's appearance seems to gradually change and then return to its original shape. But the Moon is not really changing at all. What you are seeing is the Moon being lit up by the Sun's rays in different ways on different days. What causes these differences? Changes in the positions of the Moon and Earth.

In the first phase of the Moon, called the New Moon, the giant ball of rock is not visible on Earth at all. That is because the Moon is in between the Sun and Earth. The far side of the Moon is being lit up by the Sun, but the near side is not.

The Moon's light comes from the Sun. It looks different to us on different days because the Moon and Earth are always moving.

As the Moon orbits our planet, more and more of the near side is lit up by the Sun's rays. After a few days, you can see a C-shaped sliver called a Crescent Moon. Some people think this phase of the Moon is shaped like a crescent roll.

Close to one week after you see the New Moon, the Sun lights up about half of the near side of the Moon. This phase

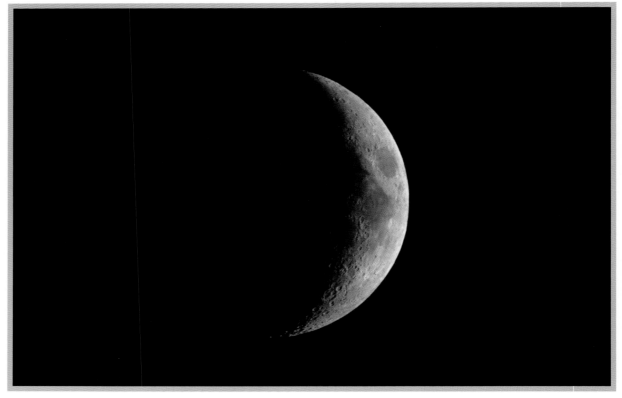

This Crescent Moon appeared 5 days after the New Moon.

is called the First Quarter Moon because the Moon is now one-quarter, or 25 percent, of the way through its full cycle.

A few days later, the Moon will have traveled far enough in its orbit for you to see a shape that has curved humps on

This stunning Full Moon appeared over gigantic rock formations called buttes in Monument Valley, which is located in Utah and Arizona.

both sides. This phase is called the Gibbous Moon because *gibbous* is the Latin word for *humped*.

Around two weeks after you see the New Moon, the Sun shines directly on the near side of the Moon. The entire Full Moon is lit up.

As the Moon continues to orbit around Earth, the Moon begins to disappear. After a few days, you will see another Gibbous Moon in the sky.

Close to three weeks after you saw the New Moon, the Sun lights up only about half of the near side of the Moon. This phase is called the Last Quarter Moon because the Moon is now just one-quarter, or 25 percent, away from completing its full cycle.

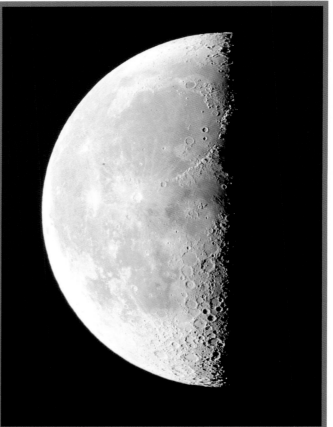

This Last Quarter Moon appeared about three weeks after the New Moon.

A few days later, all but a tiny sliver of the Crescent Moon will have disappeared. Most of the Sun's rays are now falling on the far side of the Moon.

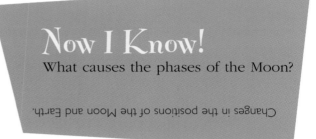

Now I Know!

What causes the phases of the Moon?

Changes in the positions of the Moon and Earth.

In just a few more days, the Moon will disappear completely. The Moon has returned to its original position in its orbital path. The far side of the Moon is fully lit up by the Sun, but the near side is in complete darkness.

The Moon has cycled through its phases for billions of years, and it will continue to do so as long as our planet and its mysterious moon exist.

 Activity

Now that you have read about the Moon's phases, it is time to observe them for yourself. All you need is a notebook and a pencil. You might also want to bring along a pair of binoculars.

During the next month, go out and look at the Moon whenever the night sky is clear. Draw a picture of what you see. As time passes, you should get a good look at all the phases of the Moon.

Look carefully with just your eyes and then by using the binoculars. Can you see any parts of the Moon that are not lit up? Be sure to include those details in your drawings.

If you have a friend who lives in another part of the country, ask him or her to do the same thing. At the end of the month, compare your results. Did you and your friend see the same thing, and at the same time of day?

 Glossary

asteroid—Small, rocky space objects that orbit the Sun. Most asteroids are located in an orbit between Mars and Jupiter. This region of the solar system is called the asteroid belt.

comet—Small icy space objects that orbit the Sun in a long, narrow orbit.

cycle—A series of steps that repeat themselves over and over again.

day—The amount of time a space object takes to rotate once. A day on Earth is twenty-four hours long, but a day on the Moon is about twenty-seven times longer.

dwarf planet—Space objects that orbit the Sun, are smaller than a planet, and are nearly round.

gravity—A force that pulls on objects. Earth's gravity prevents us from floating off into space.

orbit—To move in circles around a larger object with more gravitational pull.

phase—Stages, or steps, in a cycle.

reflect—To bounce off something or bounce back.

rotate—To spin on a central axis.

solar system—All the space objects that orbit or are influenced by our star, the Sun.

year—The amount of time it takes an object to orbit the Sun. A year on Earth is usually 365 days long. Planets that are closer to the Sun have shorter years, and planets that are farther from the Sun have longer years.

Find Out More

Books

Birch, Robin. *The Moon*. Philadelphia: Chelsea Clubhouse, 2004.

Florian, Douglas. *Comets, Stars, the Moon, and Mars: Space Poems and Paintings*. New York, Harcourt, 2007.

Klobucher, *Lisa. Earth and Earth's Moon*. Chicago: World Book, 2007.

Lilly, Melinda. *Sun and Moon*. Vero Beach, FL: Rourke, 2006.

Thimmesh, Catherine. *Team Moon: How 400,000 People Landed Apollo 11 on the Moon*. Boston: Houghton Mifflin, 2006.

Web Sites

Current Moon Phase

http://www.calculatorcat.com/moon_phases/phasenow.php

NASA Kids' Club

http://www.nasa.gov/audience/forkids/kidsclub/flash/index.html

The Moon

http://www.nineplanets.org/luna.html

Index

Page numbers for illustrations are in **boldface.**

asteroids, 10–11, **11,** 13
astronauts, 14, **14, 20,** 21
astronomers, **6**

brightness. *See* reflected light

Callisto, **13**
comets, 10–11
craters, **20**
Crescent Moon, **5, 19,** 24, **24,** 27
cycles, **6,** 6–7
 See also phases

days, 16
dwarf planets, 10–11, 13

Earth, **8, 9,** 9–10, 13–15, **16,** 23
Europa, **13**

First Quarter Moon, 25
Full Moon, **4, 25,** 26

Ganymede, **13**
Gibbous Moon, 26
gravity, 11, **12,** 13

Io, **13**

Jupiter, 9, **9,** 10, 13, **13,** 14, 19, **19,** 21

Last Quarter Moon, 26, **26**
Mars, 9, **9,** 13, 14, 19, **19,** 21
Mercury, 9, **9,** 10
moons, **13,** 13–14

Neptune, 9, **9,** 10, 13
New Moon, 23, 24, 26
nighttime, 16, **19**

orbits, 9–10, **10, 11, 12,** 15–17, 24-27

phases, **19, 22,** 23–27
planets, **9,** 9–10, **10, 12,** 13
Pluto, 10

reflected light, **5, 15,** 21, 23, **23,** 24, 27
rotation, 15–17

Saturn, 9, **9,** 13, 14, 19, 21
solar system, **9,** 9–10, **10, 12**
Sun, **9,** 9–11, **10, 11, 12,** 16–17, **18,** 19
 rays from, 21, **23,** 23–24, 26, 27

Uranus, 9, **9,** 13

Venus, 9, **9,** 19, **19,** 21

years, 9–10